The son of a village shoemaker, Joseph Stalin became absolute dictator of the largest empire in the world. Even as a schoolboy he displayed the qualities of ruthlessness and cunning which were to bring him to his position of power.

A communist dedicated to smashing the Czarist autocracy, Stalin spent much of his youth in exile. Several times he escaped. As Winston Churchill later said, he was "a man of inexhaustible courage and will-power".

But the story of his rise to absolute power after the Revolution of 1917 is not just one of a forceful personality. Stalin had a hypnotic charm. Many of the people he "liquidated", some of them old comrades, refused to believe that Stalin was responsible. Some of them, after being tortured, inscribed "Long Live Stalin" on the walls of their death cells.

When Stalin died in 1953 Russia was no longer a rural backward country. It was one of the world's foremost industrial and military nations.

This new History Makers title tells the story of the man who, though responsible for this remarkable achievement, is today so often remembered only for the "Terror".

WAYLAND HISTORY MAKERS

Joseph Stalin

David Hayes and F. H. Gregory

WAYLAND PUBLISHERS LIMITED

More Wayland History Makers

The Last Czar W. H. C. Smith
Picasso David Sweetman
Goering F. H. Gregory
Hitler Matthew Holden
Al Capone Mary Letts
The Wright Brothers Russell Ash
Karl Marx Caroline Seaward
Lenin Lionel Kochan
Rommel F. H. Gregory
Jomo Kenyatta Julian Friedmann
Martin Luther King Patricia Baker
Captain Scott David Sweetman
Bismarck Richard Kisch
Cecil Rhodes Neil Bates
Cromwell Amanda Purves
The Borgias David Sweetman
Mao Tse-tung Hugh Purcell
Franco Richard Kisch

frontispiece Joseph Stalin (1879–1953).

ISBN 85340 276 0

Copyright © 1977 by Wayland (Publishers) Ltd,
49 Lansdowne Place, Hove, East Sussex
Printed in Great Britain by
Clarke, Doble & Brendon Ltd, Plymouth and London
First published in 1977 by Wayland (Publishers) Ltd
Second impression 1979

Contents

Prologue

The death of Joseph Stalin, ruler of the Soviet Union, was announced on the morning of 6th March, 1953. A radio message solemnly reported: "The heart of Joseph Vissarionovich Stalin—Lenin's comrade-in-arms and the genius-endowed continuer of his work, wise leader and teacher of the Communist Party and of the Soviet people—has ceased to beat."

Stalin had ruled the Soviet Union with an iron fist for almost thirty years. The period of his dictatorship was marked by profound changes in the nature of Russian society, and in its relation to the rest of the world.

When Stalin came to power in the 1920s Russia was still a weak and backward country. Most of the population were peasants living in the country. Her industry lay far behind her more advanced competitors. In many ways, large areas of the country had not yet entered the twentieth century.

By the time of Stalin's death all this had changed. In 1953 Russia was the second most powerful nation in the world. She was one of the few who possessed the atomic bomb. Her industry had undergone a massive development. The number of city-dwellers had multiplied, and rural life had been transformed by the introduction of machinery. The way of life of the people had changed out of all recognition.

The era of Stalin's dictatorship was also marked by the most horrific repression and violence. Millions of people died as a direct result of the policies that Stalin imposed on Russia. The victims of the mass purges and

Above Russian women hauling a raft in 1910. Although the aims of the Russian Revolution were to free peasants like these from oppression, many millions of them later suffered terribly under Stalin's regime.

the countless prisoners in the forced labour camps all owed their fate to this one man.

But the impact of Stalin was not only felt within Russia itself. In the period after the Second World War, Stalinism was extended to virtually all the countries of Eastern Europe. Dictatorships on the Russian model were forced upon the people of these lands through the terror of the political police. Individual freedom was stamped out.

In all these changes Stalin played a decisive role. The fate of this one man was closely bound up with the fate of an entire nation. When we study the period from the 1920s to the 1950s, the Soviet Union and Joseph Stalin are one and the same.

At the time of his death Stalin was in control of half of Asia and half of Europe—a total population of over 200 million. What was most remarkable about this control was its influence on the every-day lives of those who were subject to it. It was this, more than anything, which made Stalin—the "man of steel"—the most powerful man the twentieth century, and perhaps the whole of history, has yet seen.

1. A Peasant Family

In the nineteenth century Russia was culturally as well as geographically on the outskirts of Europe. While the development of industry was changing the face of Western Europe, Russia remained socially and economically primitive—a vast country of peasants living on the land. To the south of Russia lay Georgia, once a separate nation, now a part of the Russian Empire. Georgia had at different times suffered conquest by Mongols, Turks and Persians. Now she formed a backward corner of a backward empire.

About 1875 Vissarion Ivanovich Djugashvili left his native village near Tiflis, the capital of Georgia. He went to settle in Gori, a small Georgian town with the appearance of a rambling village. There he met and married a fifteen-year-old girl named Ekaterina. Both he and Ekaterina came from peasant families. Vissarion wanted to make a living as a cobbler, hoping to earn a little more than by living on the land.

The Djugashvilis set up home in a small two-roomed hovel on the outskirts of town. The interior was dark and draughty, the door let in wind and rain. There were only a few sticks of furniture on the bare brick floor. Here Ekaterina gave birth to three children, all of whom died in infancy. On 21st December, 1879, she gave birth to a fourth child, a boy. He was christened Joseph Vissarionovich Djugashvili. Later he adopted the name Joseph Stalin. The name Stalin means literally "man of steel".

Little is known about Stalin's childhood. When he

> "The Orthodox priesthood, despite its low social rank and cultural level, belonged to the hierarchy of the privileged in that it was free of compulsory military service, the head tax, and ... the whips. Only the abolition of serfdom gave the peasants access to the ranks of the priesthood, that privilege being conditioned, however, by a police limitation: in order to be appointed to a church position, a peasant's son had to have the special dispensation of the governor." *Leon Trotsky*, Stalin.

Opposite page Joseph Vissarionovich Djugashvili (Joseph Stalin) as a boy, aged 11.

9

was six or seven years old he contracted smallpox, which left his face pock-marked for the rest of his life. A second childhood illness left his left arm useless. We know little about Stalin's father, either. Vissarion's career as a cobbler was not as successful as he had hoped it would be. He became a drunkard, leaving Ekaterina with the task of supporting herself and their young son. Vissarion died in 1890. Stalin's mother earned their meagre living by sewing, baking bread and taking in washing. She lived in Georgia until her death in 1936.

Someone from Stalin's background could not have hoped for much out of life. He was one of countless millions of dismally poor people living in a remote corner of the Russian Empire. But Ekaterina had hopes for her son—she dreamed that he might one day become a priest. This seemed the most that the son of a drunken cobbler and a poor washer-woman could hope for. To start him on a religious career Ekaterina sent Joseph to the Gori church school.

At school Stalin must have become aware that he was one of the many under-privileged members of the Russian Empire. Until he went to the Gori school Stalin spoke only Georgian—his mother could not speak any Russian. Russian was the main language at the school, where only a few lessons were given in Georgian. Stalin learned Russian easily enough, but outside school he always spoke Georgian and it remained his natural language.

Stalin spent five years at the Gori school, during which time he made a good impression on his teachers. He seems to have been a dedicated pupil. His hard work and determination, as well as his good memory, made him stand out among his fellow pupils. At the end of his five years at school he did well enough to go on to the Theological Seminary at Tiflis. His mother could not afford the fees there, but the headmaster of the Gori school and the local priest managed to obtain a scholar-

"Hating his father, young Joseph loved and respected his mother Keke ... Treasuring Soso as her sole surviving child, she worked hard to support him by sewing, laundering and scrubbing floors. It was she, too, who arranged to have the boy educated for the priesthood: an ambitious goal, it seemed, for the son of poor Georgian working-class parents." *Ronald Hingley,* Joseph Stalin: Man and Legend.

10

ship for him.

As Stalin travelled to the capital of Georgia for the second stage of his education, it looked as though his mother's wish would be fulfilled. He was on the road to a good career.

Above Stalin's family, like many Russian peasants at the end of the nineteenth century, lived in rough wooden huts like these.

11

2. The Young Rebel

In 1894, the year Stalin entered the Theological Seminary of Tiflis, Czar Alexander III died. His successor was Nicholas II, a weak-willed man more interested in his family life than the government of the nation. Nicholas was a man remote from his people in a land surging with discontent. But like the Czars before him he had no intention of giving up any of his powers. He inherited the belief that he had been destined by God to remain the absolute ruler of Imperial Russia.

Opposition to the Czar came not from the desperately poor peasants but from radical intellectuals. These were the educated thinkers of Russia. They disliked the idea of a royal family ruling their country and were determined to bring about a revolution. They were a very real threat to the royal family. Nicholas' grandfather, Czar Alexander II, had been killed by a student. Vigorous police activity had failed to root out the many secret societies and revolutionary movements formed by the radicals. The most important of these underground political groups were the Marxists. They based their political beliefs on the works of the German economist and political thinker Karl Marx, who had died in 1883.

In Georgia opposition to the Czar gave rise to three movements. The most radical of these was *Messame Dassy* (The Third Group). Its members were Marxists, as well as being Georgian Nationalists. The Theological Seminary at Tiflis was the most important school in Georgia. Most of the local intellectuals were educated there. Yet the school did not have an academic atmo-

"Pupils were not allowed to read newspapers, and were even forbidden such secular literature as the novels of Tolstoy and Dostoyevsky; but they were ingenious in evading these regulations. In so doing they risked being sent to the solitary darkness of the seminary punishment cell." *Ronald Hingley*, Joseph Stalin: Man and Legend.

Opposite page The coronation of Czar Nicholas II in 1894. He was to be Russia's last Czar.

13

sphere. It was more like a monastery than a place of learning. It was run by monks, who imposed a stifling discipline on the students.

The seminary was supposed to give a training for the Orthodox priesthood, for the benefit of those who wanted to join the Russian church. But it had another purpose, too. This was to encourage the students to accept traditional Russian ideas, values and language. The effect of these policies, however, was the opposite of that intended. After a couple of years of harsh discipline and rigorous study few students retained any respect for religion. Politically, the seminary became a breeding ground for radicals and revolutionaries. A few months before Stalin arrived there the students had been on strike. The situation had been so bad that the police were called in and the seminary closed. These student rebels were strongly nationalist, and they had demanded that Georgian literature be taught in the seminary.

Below Tiflis, in Georgia, where Stalin studied at the Theological Seminary.

During his first year in the seminary Stalin was something of a romantic. He was fond of Georgian poetry and his imagination was fired by legends from Georgia's past. He was particularly impressed by Koba, the hero of a romantic Georgian novel. This Koba was the leader of a rebellious band of mountaineers who fought against the Czarist authorities. The young Stalin tried to model himself on Koba. He even adopted the name for himself and insisted that his friends call him by it.

It was probably this feeling of Georgian nationalism that drew Stalin into the rebels' camp. His attraction to socialism and his opposition to the Russian establishment must also have been deepened by his resentment of the privileged position of the gentry.

His first political activities took place within the seminary itself. He formed a secret socialist circle along with some other students. They held meetings at which papers on a political or sociological subject were read, followed by heated discussions. During these discussions Stalin revealed a part of his personality that would become all too familiar in later years. He became annoyed whenever he was defeated in debate and would harbour a personal grudge against his opponent. One of his companions wrote: "He deemed it something unnatural that any other fellow student might be a leader and organizer of the group." To put down any contender for leadership, Stalin "injected personal squabbles into the society of his friends". He seemed more interested in asserting himself as a leader than in trying to learn something through discussion and debate with others. Not surprisingly, many of the other members of the circle were unhappy about this. "Two groups, for and against Koba, formed in the course of a few years; the struggle for a cause developed into a disgusting personal squabble...."

Late in his eighteenth year Stalin joined *Messame Dassy* and became seriously involved in revolutionary politics. To the leaders of the organization an educated member was always useful. Stalin was given the job of visiting groups of workmen and giving them talks on socialism. He was respected and accepted as an authority by these working men.

During his first years at the seminary Stalin showed no great interest in his school work. Although he disliked what he was taught he was often caught reading books banned in the seminary, which he used to borrow from the public library. He read them secretly by candlelight after the lamps had been put out in his dormitory. As time went on he became more and more troublesome. He began to argue with his teachers and was reported for being disrespectful and rude. His failure to attend some examinations was the last straw. He was expelled on 29th May 1899, at the age of nineteen.

Left Russia's population at the end of the nineteenth century consisted mostly of peasants living in rural areas and working on the land. Most of them, like this old man, used primitive methods of farming.

17

3. The Underground

Throughout the nineteenth century a large number of secret and illegal political groups existed in Russia. Many of these groups could be called socialist. Although there were many disagreements between them, they did have some features in common. They sought to end autocracy (absolute government by one man) and aristocracy (government by a nobility or privileged class), and to free the lower classes from oppression. Towards the end of the nineteenth century the Marxists became the dominant group. While many other socialists hoped to encourage a peasants' revolution the Marxists planned to bring about the revolution by means of industrial working-class people.

At first the Marxists formed a group rather than an organization. The need to keep their activities secret from the police made it difficult for them to communicate with each other, so they formed separate circles under local leaders. At the turn of the century a leading Russian Marxist, Vladimir Ilyich Ulianov, better known as Lenin, set about uniting local groups to form an organized political force. As a focal point for the movement Lenin founded a secret newspaper called *Iskra* (the Spark). This was printed abroad and smuggled into Russia. Stalin became a keen reader of *Iskra* and it had a great influence upon him.

After his expulsion from the Theological Seminary Stalin had to find a way of earning a living and a place to live. He solved both problems by getting a job as a clerk at the Tiflis Observatory. The job was poorly

> **"Stalin launched strikes and taught discontented working men the tactics of revolt. When the Bolsheviks lacked funds he helped to stage bank robberies. These were highly melodramatic affairs with gun duels, prancing steeds, decoys, and hairbreadth escapes. Stalin never actually took part in them. His department was behind-the-scenes management."** *Louis Fischer*, The Life and Death of Stalin.

Opposite page Lenin in 1900. He was the leader of the earliest revolutionary groups in Russia, and was a strong influence on the young Stalin.

Right The revolutionary newspaper *Iskra*, founded by Lenin, showing a picture of the hunger and poverty afflicting Russia's peasants.

paid but included with it was a room in the Observatory. While he worked at the Observatory he continued to play an active role among the local socialists. In March 1901 Stalin's days as a part-time revolutionary

came to an end. The police began to round up the local socialists and Stalin was among those they wanted to arrest. They raided his room in the Observatory but he was away at the time and escaped imprisonment. This was a turning point in his career—from then on he became totally involved with the revolutionary cause.

Stalin was now an outlaw using false names and false passports. The organization and his comrades provided him with a simple living. He had become a professional revolutionary and his life was that of a hunted socialist agitator. He spent his time taking part in strikes, street demonstrations, secret meetings, conferences and so on.

In September 1901 Stalin became a founder and editor of an illegal socialist newspaper. The paper was called *Brdzola* (the Struggle) and was written in the

Above In 1900 Stalin was wanted for his part in revolutionary activities. This picture is from the files of the Czarist police in Tiflis.

Above A Siberian prison. Stalin spent some time in prison, but was able to carry on his revolutionary work there.

Georgian language. Stalin also wrote for the newspaper. His essays explained the views put forward in *Iskra*, particularly those of Lenin. Already Stalin was taking his lead from Lenin. He would continue to accept Lenin's authority in political matters for years to come.

By November 1901 Stalin was a member of the Social Democratic Committee of Tiflis. This was a group which led the socialist groups in the city and had a great influence on the whole of the socialist movement in the Caucasus. (The Caucasus was an area of southern Russia running from the Black Sea in the west to the

Caspian Sea in the east.) Stalin was becoming a more important figure. Shortly afterwards he left Tiflis to continue his work in Batum. But his stay there was cut short when the police finally caught up with him. On 6th April, 1902 Stalin was arrested at a meeting of the Batum Committee.

The conditions in the Russian prisons at this time were not as harsh as might be expected. Although they were sometimes cruelly treated, political prisoners usually enjoyed certain privileges. The prisons were badly run and there was little discipline. Revolutionary work was carried on in the prison cells and socialist prisoners were able to meet and continue their long debates. Indeed, prison life provided an education for many young socialists. In the prison they learned about revolutionary thought from their more experienced comrades. After years in the Tiflis Seminary Stalin could not have found prison life unduly hard. He worked and read as much as he could and became one of the chief debaters in the prison society.

After eighteen months in prison, and despite the fact that no charge had been brought against him, Stalin was deported to eastern Siberia for a period of three years. No sooner did Stalin arrive there than he began to plan his escape. Fortunately for him eastern Siberia was in chaos, due to the expected outbreak of war between Russia and Japan. This enabled the socialists to organize the escape of many of their exiled comrades. On 5th January, Stalin began his journey back in a peasant cart. During the journey across the icebound wilderness he suffered from frost-bite, but nevertheless he pushed on and reached Tiflis at the beginning of February.

In July 1903, while Stalin was still in prison, important events were taking place elsewhere. In Brussels a conference had been arranged to form a united All Russian Socialist Party. At the conference Lenin came into

"One of the few things about which we can be quite definite in speaking of [Stalin's] early revolutionary career is that he adopted Bolshevism unhesitatingly as soon as the issues in the developing intra-party dispute became clear to him." *Robert C. Tucker*, Stalin as Revolutionary, 1879–1929.

violent conflict with Martov, another leading socialist. Lenin wanted the party to consist of strictly-disciplined and highly-organized revolutionaries. Martov merely wanted the members to meet in "co-operation under the guidance of the organization". This argument produced a split among the Marxists. Two factions developed—the Bolsheviks, the "hard" socialists who sided with Lenin, and the Mensheviks, the "soft" socialists who agreed with Martov.

Soon after his return from Siberia, Stalin sided with the Bolsheviks and began to criticize the Mensheviks. By nature he belonged to the "hard" brand of revolutionaries—softness in any form was not one of his characteristics.

Right The early years of this century in Russia saw the beginnings of a popular rising that led to the Russian Revolution in 1917.

Opposite page Julius Martov (1873–1923), leader of the Mensheviks, who were politically opposed to the Bolsheviks under Lenin.

4. The First Revolution

Despite the activities of the socialists, countless Russian workers and peasants still retained their faith in the Czar. Many believed that he did not know how the people were suffering and that bad advisers were keeping the truth from him. On Sunday, 9th January, 1905, a huge crowd of workers marched in procession to the Czar's Winter Palace in St Petersburg. They wanted to deliver a humble petition for better working conditions, and to show their loyalty they carried many icons and portraits of the Czar. When they got to the Palace, however, the Czarist troops met them with bullets, killing and wounding several hundred.

This act, which became known as the massacre of "Bloody Sunday", turned the people violently against the Czar. A wave of rebellion spread throughout the Russian Empire. In the industrial areas the workers went on strike, while in the countryside the peasants turned on their landlords, seizing their land and livestock. The streets were full of demonstrators, and the socialists at last emerged from hiding. In St. Petersburg and Moscow the workers formed their own alternative governments, known as *soviets*.

For the Czar this was a desperate situation. The greater part of the Russian army was involved in a war with Japan and had suffered a number of disastrous defeats. In Odessa the crew of the warship *Potemkin* mutinied and joined the revolt. The position of the Czar was not strong enough to stop the revolution by force.

Lenin was later to call the revolution of 1905 "the

> **"By 1905, Stalin's drive as an organizer had earned him his spurs in the Bolshevik party, many of whose leaders were in Siberian prisons or foreign exile; he became a medium-sized fish in a small pond."**
> *Louis Fischer*, The Life and Death of Stalin.

Opposite page After the massacre of "Bloody Sunday" in 1905, protest meetings became regular. This picture shows police and soldiers breaking up one such meeting.

Above A strike in the city of Kharkhov on 9th July, 1905. The demonstrations of this time amounted to a minor revolution.

general rehearsal" for the successful revolution of 1917. But there were great contrasts between them. The first revolution was a spontaneous revolt, unplanned and unorganized. With the exception of Leon Trotsky, who led the Petersburg soviet, the major socialist leaders did not play a great role in shaping the course of the revolution. Lenin himself did not return to Russia from his Swiss exile until nine months after the events of Bloody Sunday, by which time the Czar was in a much stronger position.

Stalin himself played no national role in the first revolution but continued his local activities and his revolutionary journalism. The tremendous upheaval going on around him seemed to pass him by and had little effect on him. Trotsky later said of him: "Unable to catch fire himself, he was incapable of inflaming others." Trotsky also offered another explanation for Stalin's lack of action during the first revolution:

Above the first meeting of Lenin and Stalin in Finland in December 1905.

"Whenever he feels himself ignored or neglected, he is inclined to turn his back upon developments as well as upon people, creep into a corner, moodily pull out his pipe and dream of revenge. That was why in 1905 he walked into the shadows with hidden resentment and became something in the nature of an editor."

But Stalin's position was not an easy one, for he was alone in his views. The Mensheviks were the majority party in the Caucasus. Most of the Bolsheviks—Stalin's party—wanted to join with the Mensheviks. Stalin was almost alone in supporting Lenin's ideas and in his strong criticism of the Mensheviks.

In October 1905 the Czar established a *Duma* (Elected Assembly) and granted freedom of the press. These moves satisfied the moderate supporters of the revolution and the extremists were left to stand alone. The end of the war with Japan, despite the unfavourable terms of the peace treaty, also helped the Czar. The

"From the democratic revolution we shall begin straightaway within the measure of our strength ... to pass to the socialist revolution. We stand for uninterrupted revolution. We will not stop halfway." *Lenin, September 1905.*

29

army remained faithful and when the workers attempted armed risings in a number of cities they were firmly put down. Gradually the revolution lost impetus. By 1907 the Czar had the reins of power firmly in his hands once more.

Towards the end of 1907, when the tide of revolution was at a low ebb, Stalin was in the city of Baku, on the Persian border. Baku was a great centre of the oil industry and at the time was beset by labour troubles in which Stalin played a significant role. He wrote a series of articles in the news-sheet of the Bolshevik trade unionists. He was well aware that the oil workers' strike would not change the course of the revolution—this was one of the last battles. But it did bring him into the public eye. As one commentator put it: "The dead silence in the rest of Russia was the sounding board on which the 'signal' from Baku reverberated with unusual strength."

With the power of the Czar largely re-established, the publicity had its disadvantages. Stalin was arrested for a second time. He spent the next few years continually in and out of prison. Despite this he was still able to contribute articles to the journals of the Bolsheviks. He had made a reputation for himself as one of the leading figures in the party in the Caucasus, and he had already been brought to the attention of Lenin.

In 1913, however, Stalin was again arrested in St Petersburg. This time his banishment lasted a full four years. It was during this spell that he heard of the outbreak of World War One. Exiled in the Siberian wilderness, these were perhaps the least eventful and most peaceful years of Stalin's life. But the revolution of 1917 began for Stalin a new period of intense political activity.

Opposite page Stalin (marked with a white cross) on his way to Siberia in 1913, after being deported by the Czarist authorities.

5. The End of Czardom

As the fateful year of 1917 dawned, all areas of Russian society were exhausted by over two years of all-out war. The vast Russian army had suffered seven million dead, wounded or missing. Behind the battle-lines, towns and villages throughout the country were ravaged by disease, famine and desperate poverty. The weak Czarist regime could not meet the demands of its people for "peace, land and bread".

In February 1917 riots and demonstrations broke out in Petrograd, the Russian capital. These soon spread to the other main towns. Throughout the country the people set up *soviets*, or local parliaments, to represent their interests. In the face of a massive wave of popular opposition to his rule, the Czar, Nicholas II, had no choice but to resign. On 3rd March the Romanov dynasty, which had ruled over Russia for centuries, finally came to an end. In its place a Provisional Government composed mainly of moderate Liberals took over the administration of the country and the conduct of the war.

Most of the revolutionary leaders were now far from the centre of action. The spontaneous revolution had taken them by surprise. Many were in exile abroad, or imprisoned in Siberia. Before the revolution, the worsening military situation had led the Czarist authorities to send even their political prisoners to the front. Stalin, however, was declared unfit for military service, due to the defect in his left arm which he had had since childhood. When the old order was toppled, and the

> **"Any day, if not today or tomorrow, the crash of the whole of European imperialism may come. The Russian revolution ... has begun it and opened a new epoch. Hail the world-wide socialist revolution."** *Lenin, 3rd April, 1917.*

Opposite page The First World War took a terrible toll on the lives of Russian soldiers. This picture shows dead bodies laid out in the snow.

Above Lenin stating his thesis on 3rd April, 1917, after his return from exile in Switzerland.

political prisoners released, Stalin became one of the first senior Bolsheviks to arrive in Petrograd.

As a member of the Central Committee of the Bolshevik party, Stalin briefly assumed the post of editor of its paper, *Pravda*. Until the return of Lenin from Switzerland on 3rd April, the leadership of the Bolsheviks was in the joint hands of Stalin and Kamenev. The Bolsheviks were at this time still a fairly small and powerless group. The membership was divided into various factions which vied for control. Stalin, true to his nature, took up a middle-of-the-road position on the major issues of the day. His articles and speeches on topics such as the party's attitude to the new government and to the soviets reflected his desire always to keep a foot in each camp.

When Lenin arrived in Petrograd, Stalin withdrew behind the scenes. As yet, Lenin's policy of opposition to the Provisional Government was not popular within

the party. But throughout April 1917 Lenin gradually won acceptance for his idea of a direct seizure of power. Only then did Stalin openly support him.

The national conference of the Bolsheviks at the end of April elected a new Central Committee of which both Lenin and Stalin were members. Since the February Revolution the party had more than doubled in size, and the 133 delegates at this conference now represented about 75,000 members. But although the party was swelling rapidly in numbers, it was still not strong enough to attempt to seize power.

During May and June 1917 the revolutionary spirit of the people of Petrograd steadily mounted. The government was forced to maintain a delicate balance between the competing parties and groups. The Bolsheviks were careful, however, not to damage their cause by premature action.

In July, the revolutionary wave temporarily subsided,

Above Lenin addressing the first All Russian Congress of Soviets in 1917.

"We need a force of armed workers connected with the main revolutionary centres.... Revolution cannot win without an armed force at its disposal." *Stalin, 12th March, 1917.*

35

and Lenin was forced into hiding. Once again, Stalin stepped forward to lead the party in Lenin's absence. During this period, the Bolsheviks were being attacked from all sides and were even blamed for the military failures at the front. Stalin published an appeal to the party to "close the ranks", in which he warned of the dangers of counter-revolution and instructed the members of the party to "prepare for the coming battles".

The value of such a warning was shown at the end of August, when a right-wing attempt by General Kornilov to take power was narrowly defeated. This defeat gave the Bolsheviks the impetus they needed for their last lap on the road to power. Their reputation among the people was increasing and they gradually became the majority party in many of the soviets.

Finally, on 25th October, 1917, Lenin and the Bolsheviks undertook an all-out assault on the Provisional Government's seat of power. The government was by this time virtually without support, and little violence was needed to establish the new rulers.

In the final days of the upheaval, Stalin seemed to play little part. He was even absent from the meeting of the Bolshevik Central Committee on the morning of the uprising. As usual, he did not wish openly to commit himself to a definite policy until he knew whether it would succeed or not. As Trotsky wrote later, "In the event of failure he could always tell Lenin and me: 'It's all your fault!' " But in the end this evasiveness would serve to help, rather than hinder, Stalin's career.

> **"All this points to the necessity of interpreting the principle of self-determination as a right not of the bourgeoisie, but of the working masses of a given nation. The principle of self-determination must be an instrument in the struggle for socialism and must be subordinated to the principle of socialism."** *Stalin, report to 3rd All-Russian Congress of Soviets, 1918.*

Opposite page Stalin speaking at the 6th Congress of the Russian Social Democratic Labour Party in August 1917. Although Stalin now held considerable power in the Bolshevik party, he kept in the background during the October Revolution of 1917.

6. Red Versus White

The actual seizure of power in October 1917 by the Bolsheviks was a fairly bloodless event. But this "October Revolution" did not put an end to the sufferings of the war. On the contrary, it was followed by three more years of bitter and bloody conflict. Only at the end of this period of civil war and foreign intervention had the Bolsheviks finally secured their position as the unchallenged rulers of Russian society.

In the first Soviet Government, Stalin was appointed to the post of Commissar of Nationalities. In 1913 Stalin had, with Lenin's approval, drafted the Bolsheviks' policy statement on the question of national self-rule, and now he had the chance to turn theory into practice.

Stalin's first act was to travel to Helsinki to announce the granting of independence to Finland, which up until now had been a part of the Russian Empire. Similar measures led to the creation of national governments in the borderlands of Russia. Most of these were, however, hostile to the Bolsheviks. The danger of a break-up of Russia into a number of independent nation states led the Bolsheviks to reverse their policy of supporting national self-rule.

In Bolshevik eyes, the necessities of the Civil War demanded ruthless and centralized control. There would be little room in future for national independence. As Stalin declared forcefully in May 1918, the Bolsheviks wanted "a strong Russia-wide state authority capable of conclusively quelling the enemies of socialism and of organizing a new, communist economy".

At the start of the Civil War the main dilemma facing the Bolsheviks was whether to continue the war with Germany. They were in a weak bargaining position against the might of the Imperial German Army. The peace negotiations which took place at Brest-Litovsk finally produced a settlement which conceded huge areas of territory and raw materials to Germany. A fierce argument raged within the party over whether to accept the terms or whether to fight on. Stalin followed Lenin in supporting this settlement.

The Bolsheviks had hoped that their example would be the spark that would ignite the flame of revolution in the West. But it was not to be. Instead they were faced

Above The negotiations at Brest–Litovsk, during which the Bolsheviks made several concessions to Germany. Lenin was severely attacked by Trotsky for his actions, but he had the support of Stalin.

> **"To unite locally the workers of all nationalities of Russia into single, integral collective bodies, to unite these collective bodies into a single party—such is the task."**
> *Stalin*, Marxism and the National Question (*1913*).

with the prospect of defending their regime alone against the "White" armies inside Russia and from the invading Allied forces. In the spring and summer of 1918 the White armies, headed by ex-Czarist officers, occupied vital strategic centres in Siberia. An anti-Soviet regional government headed by Admiral Kolchak was set up at Omsk. Meanwhile, the Cossack forces led by General Krasnov attempted to drive north from their base in the Ukraine and in the Volga region to link up with their White allies. The Bolshevik regime was in deep crisis. Nearly all members of the govern-

ment left Moscow in order to be near the front line.

Stalin went to the town of Czaritsyn (later re-named Stalingrad) on the river Volga, in order to arrange the movement of grain to Moscow, which was threatened with starvation. The rail link between the two towns, which had carried most of Moscow's food supply, had been cut by the advancing White legions. Stalin, faced with problems of greedy merchants and chaotic distribution, imposed rationing of food and control of prices. In the task of re-organization he proved himself a capable and determined administrator. "I am driving

Above A street scene in Petrograd during the October Revolution of 1917. The Russian Revolution changed the country's history and opened the way for Stalin to make his move for power.

> **"Although Stalin acquired valuable military experience in the Civil War, he did not emerge from it with a party reputation for having a first-class military mind. He was not one of the principal organizers of the Red Army, nor did he show the qualities of an outstanding military leader."** *Robert C. Tucker*, Stalin as Revolutionary, 1879–1929.

and scolding everyone who needs it," he reported to Lenin, who had remained in the Kremlin during the Civil War. "You may be sure that we will spare no one, neither ourselves nor others, and we will, no matter what, deliver the grain."

Stalin's promise was eventually fulfilled, but it was not until October 1918 that the White Army besieging Czaritsyn was finally repulsed. The credit for this success was a matter of bitter dispute between Stalin and

Right Czar Nicholas II with his three daughters under arrest in 1918. The Czar and his family were murdered by the revolutionaries not long after this picture was taken.

Trotsky, now the commander of the Red Army. Stalin had openly sympathized with a group of Red officers who had refused to obey the orders of certain ex-Czarist generals and military experts whom Trotsky had placed at the head of the Red Army. This "Czaritsyn group" claimed the responsibility for the victory over the Whites, but Trotsky disputed their version of events. He claimed that the command of the southern front, not the defenders of Czaritsyn, had made the important breach in the ring of White armies. The squabble between the two Bolshevik leaders, who had always shared a deep personal animosity, was an ominous foretaste of things to come.

The Civil War reached its peak in 1919. The White Armies, supported by British and French forces, threatened to engulf both Petrograd and Moscow. But by November 1919 the Whites were in retreat on all fronts. The victory of the Soviet regime was secured. The following year both Stalin and Trotsky were awarded the Order of the Red Banner for their part in defending the new system.

At the end of the Civil War, the power of the Bolshevik (now re-named the Communist) Party had been consolidated. But the whole country was even more exhausted by its efforts. Industrial production had collapsed, and the country was threatened by famine. An enormous task of re-organization was needed. The Communists offered strong and often repressive leadership to get the country back on its feet after almost ten years of war. In this effort Stalin had a crucial role to play. While Lenin was alive, however, Stalin was very much a secondary figure. His abilities as an administrator were recognized, but few regarded him as a potential leader of the party and of the country.

But although the spotlight was not yet on him, Stalin was prepared to wait patiently in the wings.

> "When the Order of the Red Banner began to be awarded in the Civil War, and had been given to Trotsky, Kamenev proposed that Stalin should receive it too. Kalinin asked in surprise, 'For what?' Bukharin intervened: 'Can't you understand? This is Lenin's idea. Stalin cannot live unless he has what someone else has. He will never forgive it.'" *Robert Conquest*, The Great Terror.

7. Top of the Pyramid

Even while Lenin remained the active leader of the country, Stalin was able to hold tremendous power in his own hands. Under the very noses of his rivals, yet hardly noticed by them, Stalin rose to supremacy within the party and the government. "Two years after the end of the civil war", Stalin's biographer Isaac Deutscher writes, "Russian society already lived under Stalin's virtual rule without being aware of the ruler's name." While his fellow Communist leaders concerned themselves with the finer points of theory, doctrine and principle, the practical day-to-day running of the country gradually fell into Stalin's hands. An enormous central government machine was emerging in Russia. Stalin, almost without anybody noticing it, established himself at its centre.

Stalin held three highly important offices. Firstly, as Commissar of Nationalities, he came to deal with the affairs of nearly half the entire population of the country. The Soviet Union was composed of a mixture of peoples of different nationalities. Nearly 65 million of the 140 million inhabitants of the Soviet Union were not of Russian origin.

Secondly, as Commissar of the Workers and Peasants Inspectorate, a body set up to control every branch of the administration, Stalin came to supervise the whole of the government machine, from top to bottom.

Thirdly, as a member of the *Politbureau*, the "real government of the country", Stalin had a direct influence on the conduct and direction of policy. Through-

"Stalin won both because of his skill in manipulating the party machine which he controlled, and also because he succeeded in convincing many—probably a real and large majority—of Party members that his methods and policies could cope with the many problems of the time." *Alec Nove*, Stalinism and After.

Opposite page The Russian Revolution did not solve all of Russia's problems. There was still high unemployment throughout the country; this picture shows a crowd of unemployed at a railway station in 1919.

out the Civil War, the *Politbureau* consisted of five men—Lenin, Trotsky, Stalin, Kamenev and Bukharin. Stalin acted as the liaison officer between this body and the Organization Bureau, another committee which dealt with party affairs. By developing his influence in all these branches of government, Stalin alone came to act as the crucial link in the chain of party, state and the country as a whole.

Yet more power came to Stalin through his appointment in April 1922 to the post of General Secretary of the Central Committee of the Communist Party. More and more it was the single figure of Stalin on whom the running of the country depended. Stalin himself expressed his ambitions in the following way to a group of supporters: "Don't forget we are living in Russia, the land of the Czars. The Russian people like to have one man standing at the head of the state." It was clear that Stalin saw himself in that leading position.

In March 1923 Lenin suffered a stroke which left him paralysed and incapable of any political activity. The loss of the "Father of the Revolution" triggered off a long struggle among the leading contenders for power. Stalin, who had always walked in Lenin's shadow and had followed the guidelines laid down by him, was already in a position to secure the leadership for himself. Long before Lenin's death in January 1924 Stalin had begun to take steps to defeat his rivals.

Like a deadly game of musical chairs, the inner-party conflicts continued throughout the 1920s. Not until 1929 was Stalin the undisputed dictator of Russia. Yet in this period Stalin always seemed to be one up on his rivals. He proved himself a master of timing and tactical sense. In the words of another biographer, Stalin was "a first-rate tactician in the intrigues of party machinery".

For a number of years, Stalin had recognized Trotsky

> "Trotsky underestimated Stalin and regarded him as a 'provincial'. But the provincial, with a sharp eye to the future, took the job of General Secretary of the Communist Party. ... Lenin dominated the party, and the secretary was a subordinate. But Stalin understood that in a highly centralized state controlled by the party the General Secretary would be a key man after Lenin's death. Meanwhile the position enabled Stalin to work assiduously and in the dark gathering a band of henchmen who would be loyal to him because he appointed them and could dismiss them." *Louis Fischer,* The Life and Death of Stalin.

> "[Stalin] is an unprincipled intriguer who subordinates everything to the preservation of his power. He changes theories depending on whom he wants to get rid of at the moment." *Bukharin, 1928.*

as his main enemy and as the other chief contender for the leadership. Stalin, therefore, allied with two other members of the Politbureau, Kamenev and Zinoviev, in order to defeat the claims of Trotsky and his "Left Opposition". This alliance made constant attacks on Trotsky in the party at meetings and in the press. Stalin also began to appoint his friends and followers to the lower offices of the party. In this way he slowly deprived Trotsky of any real power-base from which he could

> **"Stalin took possession of power ... with an impersonal machine. It was not that he created the machine, but the machine that created him."** *Trotsky* Stalin.

Left Leon Trotsky in 1920. At first a very powerful man in the revolutionary organization, Stalin gradually wore down his power and eventually had him expelled from Russia.

> **"The task of the Party is to bury Trotskyism as an ideology."** *Stalin, 1925.*

47

launch a counter-assault. After a lengthy struggle, Trotsky was forced to relinquish his position in the party heirarchy. In October 1926 Trotsky was expelled from the Politbureau, and in December 1927 he was forcibly exiled.

After the defeat of Trotsky, Stalin turned on his former supporters. New members were asked to join the Politbureau to strengthen Stalin's position. Stalin now sided with Bukharin, Tomsky and Rykov in the Politbureau and successfully eliminated Kamenev and Zinoviev, who had allied with him against Trotsky.

But once again, as soon as he was successful in this campaign, Stalin callously betrayed his followers. Throughout 1928 and 1929 Stalin worked to undermine the influence of his rivals. Rykov was removed as head of the Soviet Union. Tomsky was ousted as leader of the trade unions and Bukharin was dismissed both from the Politbureau and from his position as head of the Communist International.

Right Mikhail Tomsky, one of the men whom Stalin used to help him to power. Once he had served his purpose, Stalin got rid of him.

So by the end of 1929 Stalin was the absolute ruler of the party and the country. No member of the Polit-bureau would any longer dare to challenge his authority. In his rise to power he had shown great determination and ruthlessness. It was not just jealousy that made Bukharin exclaim that Stalin was a "small-minded, malicious man—no, not a man, but a devil!" But the propaganda machine announced that "Stalin is the Lenin of today". Within Russia, Stalin had reached the top of the pyramid. But his main achievements still lay in the future.

Below Lenin lying in state in January 1924. With Lenin now dead and his rivals eliminated, Stalin had achieved his ambition to become the absolute ruler of Russia.

8. Socialism in One Country

During the 1920s in Russia there was constant argument among those in power. This was not only about who should be in control of the one-party state that had developed. It also concerned the kinds of policies that would affect the country at large.

The policy that aroused most argument was Stalin's idea of "socialism in one country". Marx, Lenin and the early communists had worked on the principle that socialism was an international movement. They believed that no socialist country could survive on its own for a long time surrounded by hostile capitalist states.

But as early as 1924, Stalin came to challenge this belief. His theory was that Russia was capable of surviving and prospering as a socialist country without foreign help. This theory, even though it seemed to disagree with the internationalist principles of the socialist movement, came to be accepted by all.

It was obvious to Stalin, however, that for Russia to survive on its own, the economy of the country would have to be strong and self-sufficient. For this reason, in 1929 he began a massive programme to industrialize Russia. In due course, this "second revolution" would transform Russia from a backward country dependent on farming into a modern industrial society.

The major task at hand was to unite the efforts of Russia's farmers. Millions of poor peasants had owned their land independent of each other. Each farmer could only barely survive through his own efforts. The

> **"Now there stands before us a new task—the industrialization of our country. The most serious difficulties have been left behind. Is it possible to doubt that we shall be equal to this new task, the industrialization of our country? Of course not!"**
> *Stalin, speech to Party meeting in Leningrad, April 1926.*

Opposite page In 1929 Stalin launched a programme of industrial and agricultural development in Russia. This steel works at Magnitogorsk was one of the results of the new drive.

Above Leningrad workers with their new tractor.

"**Breakneck industrialization, with priority for heavy industry, and forcible mass collectivization of the peasantry would be the twin hallmarks of the revolution from above that Stalin inaugurated in 1929.... The strategy succeeded, but not without a protracted struggle in the party, one of the bitterest battles of Stalin's career.**" *Robert C. Tucker*, Stalin as Revolutionary, 1879–1929.

plan begun in 1929 was designed to "pool" these individual farms into large "collectives" farms, which the government would supply with money and machinery. In this way it would be possible for the farmers to survive in a more efficient way. It would also allow them to supply a steady quantity of grain for the growing populations of the industrial towns.

At first this plan was fairly successful. But about the middle of 1929 the success of the policy seemed to make Stalin over-enthusiastic about the possibilities of collective farms. He ordered that *all* peasants should be forced to join collectives. This meant that even the richer peasants, the so-called "kulaks", were to have their farms merged. Many of them resisted violently the attempts of the government to seize their land and

Above The first workers on the Magnitogorsk steel works lived in mud huts like this one.

belongings. A bitter struggle began. The forceful resistance of the peasants was met with severe repression. But many peasants still refused to submit. Instead they slaughtered their cattle and burned their crops in protest at the policy. Villages were surrounded and forced to surrender at machine-gun point.

The results of this second "civil war" were devastating. Over half of the country's livestock—cattle, sheep, goats and horses—was slaughtered by the desperate peasants. Famine once again became widespread. But the policy was forced through despite this resistance. By 1932 three-fifths of all farms had become collectives.

This agricultural revolution was accompanied by an attempt to expand Russia's limited industry. The production of machinery, the building of oil wells and the

"This era in which we live ... will be known in history as the era of Stalin, just as the preceding era entered history as the time of Lenin."
Kamenev, at the 11th congress of the CPSU, 1934.

introduction of electricity all proceeded at a terrific pace.

In terms of statistics, the success of this industrial development could not be doubted. Under the so-called "five-year plans", industrial output continued to expand by leaps and bounds. Between 1932 and 1937, during the second such plan, the annual rate of increase in industrial production was nearly 14%. Stalin's belief in Russia's potential to become a leading industrial nation seemed to be well justified.

But against the great strides forward taken in modernizing the country during this period must be set the immense cost in terms of human life and suffering that they brought about. Forced labour and starvation were the fate of many of the peasants who had resisted collectivization, and they were degraded virtually to the status of slaves. The workers who developed the gigantic new iron and coal mines, and who built the blast furnaces and power stations, suffered great hardship in the process. Severe penalties were imposed on absentees and "slackers". A rigid wage system was introduced which rewarded the workers whose production levels were highest. These workers were glorified as national heroes. The vast majority of workers, however, had to endure low wages and harsh conditions.

In Stalin's Russia there was a total absence of political freedom. Stalin was the "great dictator" who was unopposed in the party, in the government and in the country as a whole. This was the price the Russian people had to pay for "socialism in one country".

Opposite page Stalin's "five-year plans" inspired the Russian people to furious activity, but they were also subjected to very poor treatment in order to make them achieve the targets set. This picture shows young people working in the Kemerovo region in 1931.

9. The Great Terror

On 1st December, 1934, Stalin's friend and colleague Sergei Kirov was assassinated in Leningrad. Kirov had been a member of the Politbureau and the head of the Communist Party in Leningrad. In itself a fairly minor event, this act was to have terrifying effects. Stalin used it as an excuse to begin to wipe out the "old guard" of the Bolsheviks.

Throughout the 1930s a series of "show trials" and mass purges took place of those people whom Stalin regarded as a potential threat to his power. Exactly how many died in these purges may never be known. As many as one million present and former party members died in the purges. But in the population as a whole, the Great Terror, as it became known, claimed well over ten million victims.

Many of the original leaders of the party—including Zinoviev, Kamenev and Bukharin—found themselves on trial. They were charged with many crimes, such as plotting industrial sabotage, collaborating with Trotsky to restore capitalism in the Soviet Union and planning to kill Stalin himself. These charges were, of course, made up by Stalin and his henchmen. They were designed to give an appearance of legality to Stalin's actions.

Many of those who were tried were, however, made to confess to these non-existent crimes. The trials were stage-managed so that the maximum publicity could be given to the regime in its open exposure of the "traitors". Those defendants who did "confess" did so

> **"To choose one's victims, to prepare one's plans minutely, to slake an implacable vengeance, and then to go to bed ... there is nothing sweeter in the world."** *Stalin, quoted in Boris Souvarine,* Stalin.

Opposite page Stalin in one of his favourite poses.

Above In the 1930s Stalin continued his campaign to destroy all possible opposition. This picture shows one of the "trials" at which many of his enemies were condemned to death without a fair hearing.

"[Stalin] seeks to strike, not at the ideas of his opponent, but at his skull." *Trotsky, 1936.*

in hope of mercy. Those who refused were tried in private. In the end, most of the major defendants were executed, while others escaped with long prison sentences.

There was one man whom Stalin could not bring to trial—his old adversary Trotsky. The latter, hounded out of Russia, continued to organize opposition to Stalin among his tiny band of followers. But even though he was exiled in Mexico, he could not escape Stalin's grasp. In 1940 an agent of Stalin murdered Trotsky in his home by smashing his skull with an ice-pick.

But Trotsky, although absent from the trials, was in fact the main defendant. He was accused of organizing an international plot to destroy the Soviet state—and

Left Grigori Zinoviev. Once a supporter of Stalin, Zinoviev was executed in 1936.

he was finally sentenced to death in his absence. Many of the lesser-known defendants were forced to admit openly to their part in this imaginary plot.

In August 1936 Zinoviev and Kamenev, who had been deported to Siberia four years previously, were tried and executed along with fourteen other prominent Bolsheviks. The following year, another major show trial was staged, with executions to follow. In addition, a secret trial of some of the highest generals in the Red Army resulted in more mass executions. Finally, in March 1938, a further show trial convicted the remaining well-known Bolsheviks such as Rykov and Bukharin.

The great show trials and executions of the 1930s

"By exterminating without any mercy these spies, provocateurs, wreckers, and diversionists, the Soviet land will move even more rapidly along the Stalinist route, socialist culture will flourish even more richly, the life of the Soviet people will become even more joyous." Pravda, *10th March, 1938.*

were only a part of Stalin's plan to destroy all actual or potential political opposition to his dictatorship. Apart from these, mass purges and executions were carried out against people at all levels of the social scale. These took place with almost no publicity and often without any trials at all. The Soviet secret police (the NKVD), under their chiefs Yagoda, Yezhov and Berya arrested and deported millions of civilians. By these means Stalin sent millions of people—ordinary workers and peasants, intellectuals, party officials, civil servants

Right Alexei Rykov, another former supporter of Stalin and victim of a show trial in 1938.

and military experts—to their deaths. Countless more were sent to slave labour camps.

The result of these purges was to strengthen Stalin's iron grip on the Soviet state and society. Nobody from the highest party official to the poorest peasant was safe from the Great Terror that enveloped Russia.

Stalin was successful in his aim to root out and destroy all those who would not give blind obedience to his regime and adulation to himself. The great dictator had reached the height of his powers.

Left Nikolai Bukharin who, with Alexei Rykov, was condemned to death in a show trial in 1938.

"In 1928 and 1929, Stalin, reckoning with possible indignation in the party and country, did not dare shoot Trotsky. In 1936, Zinoviev and Kamenev were executed. That is an index to the crescendo of terror during the seven intervening years. In retrospect the 1920s in Russia were an era of freedom compared with the political pogroms of the 1930s and the rigours of the '40s and '50s. Stalin advanced towards absolutism slowly." *Louis Fischer*, The Life and Death of Stalin.

10. The German Menace

During the 1930s the main object of Stalin's foreign policy was to gain valuable time to allow his massive re-armaments programme to take place. Russia needed to maintain peace abroad at all costs, since the country was not yet strong enough to fight another major war.

Stalin explained Russia's position in 1931: "We are fifty to a hundred years behind the advanced countries," he declared. "We must make good this lag in ten years. Either we do it or they will crush us."

The rise of the Nazis to power in Germany in 1933 created a problem for Stalin. He watched with growing concern Hitler's attempts to control Austria and Czechoslovakia. It was clear that Hitler's aims were a threat to the balance of power in Europe. The growth of German strength brought with it a threat of war.

Stalin knew that Hitler's aims included the destruction of the Soviet Union and the takeover of much of its territory. He had to choose whether to ally himself with the Western democracies—Britain and France—against Hitler, or whether to seek a temporary agreement with Germany.

Hitler and Stalin both knew that at some stage war between their countries was likely if not inevitable. But Hitler first wanted to settle accounts with the West before turning his attention to Russia. And although Stalin wanted to keep open the option of an agreement with Britain and France, he was anxious for a non-aggression pact with Germany. This would give him a much-needed breathing-space in which to complete his

"At present [the British and French] are again trying to push the Soviet Union into a war against Germany. This policy had very bad consequences for Russia in 1914. It is in the interests of both Germany and Russia to avoid a mutual massacre for the benefit of the Western democracies." *von Schulenberg (German Ambassador in Moscow) to Molotov, 15th August, 1939.*

Opposite page Russian soldiers fighting in Finland in 1939.

RIBBENTROP

STALIN

Above Molotov, the Russian
Foreign Minister, and
Ribbentrop, the Foreign
Minister of Germany, sign the
non-aggression pact between
Stalin and Hitler in August
1939. A week later, Hitler
invaded Poland and provoked
the beginning of the Second
World War.

re-armaments programme.

By now Hitler had occupied Czechoslovakia, and he
was preparing to invade Poland. Before doing so, he
wanted to make sure that Stalin would not side with
the West. After rather half-hearted efforts on both sides,
the failure of the communist East and the capitalist
West to come to an agreement left the field open for
the Stalin–Hitler non-aggression pact of August 1939.

This pact, finally agreed between the Foreign
Minister of each country, Molotov and Ribbentrop,
gave Hitler a free hand in the West. A secret clause provided for the division of Poland, the Baltic States and
Finland between Russia and Germany. Only a week

after it was signed Poland was invaded by Germany, and this act was met by a declaration of war by Britain on Germany. The Second World War had begun.

What did Stalin hope to gain from the non-aggression pact? It is debatable whether he thought that war with Germany could be postponed indefinitely or whether it could merely be prevented for a few years. In any case, the pact allowed Russia to continue to rebuild her industry and defences, and to prepare for full-scale war.

Germany's lightning victory over Poland filled Stalin with worry. He feared that Hitler would break their agreement and attack Russia immediately. The refusal of the Finns to grant Russia the use of military bases,

Above Russian heavy artillery on its way to the front.

needed for the defence of Leningrad, gave Stalin an excuse to attack Finland—ironically, the very country to which Stalin himself had been authorized to grant independence over twenty years before. In March 1940 the war was successfully completed. Soon after, the French defence against the Nazi invaders collapsed, and Britain withdrew her forces from the Continent.

The sweeping successes of the German army encouraged Stalin to force the Baltic States—Estonia, Latvia and Lithuania—to become part of the Soviet Union in order to strengthen its defences. Diplomatic negotiations between Russia and Germany continued. Although the appearance of friendship was maintained, it was obvious that tension was mounting. Hitler gradually extended his control southwards into the Balkans.

The expectation of war led Stalin to make a non-aggression pact with Japan. He did not want to fight a war on two fronts.

Finally, on 22nd June, 1941, Hitler's forces began the "second front" with their invasion of Russia. Astonishingly, Stalin had been repeatedly warned by his advisers that Hitler was planning this operation, yet he ignored their warnings. Only a week before the invasion, he had denied the rumours of a coming war.

Whether Stalin's denial was sincere or not is an open question. But he was certainly realistic enough to know that at some stage Russia would have to defend herself from attack. The German invasion made Stalin a war leader as well as the leader of the country. In the following months and years, the system he had fashioned would be severely tested as never before.

Opposite page As Hitler's army moved towards the Russian border, Russian troops prepared to defend their country.

11. The Commander

Stalin's immediate reaction to the news of the German attack was one of acute embarrassment. Since the completion of the non-aggression pact, he had taken care to keep peace with Hitler as much as possible. "The friendship of the peoples of Germany and the Soviet Union," he had written to Hitler, "cemented by blood, has every reason to be lasting and firm." But now the two dictators were locked in a life-or-death struggle.

As supreme commander of the Red Army, Stalin divided the enormous front into three sectors, each commanded by a single general. The State Defence Committee, consisting of five members—Stalin, Molotov, Voroshilov, Berya and Malenkov—was to conduct the direction of the war effort.

The steady advance of the Nazis in the early stages of the war created panic behind the Russian lines. A run of Russian defeats caused desperation in the Kremlin. Nearly the whole of the Ukraine was held by the Nazis; Leningrad had been cut off and blockaded. Stalin dismissed and replaced his commanders, Voroshilov and Budienny. They were old members of the "Czaritsyn group" that had been the cause of his earlier quarrel with Trotsky.

In October 1941 Hitler launched an attempt to encircle and capture Moscow. At one point his troops were within five miles of the city. All government departments were evacuated and many archives burned. Stalin, however, remained in the Kremlin throughout the war. He never visited the front to inspire his troops.

> **"Not a single step backward.... You have to fight to your last drop of blood to defend every position, every foot of Soviet territory."** *Stalin's Order of the Day, 28th July, 1942.*

Opposite page Defences on the outskirts of Moscow in 1941.

"All the peoples of the Soviet Union have risen as one to defend their motherland, rightly considering the present Patriotic War the common cause of all working people, irrespective of nationality or religion." *Stalin, on 26th anniversary of October Revolution* (1943).

"Stalingrad signified the decline of the German fascist army. As is well known, the Germans were unable to recover after the Stalingrad slaughter." *Stalin, on 26th anniversary of October Revolution (1943).*

"It was against the background of this battle [i.e. Stalingrad], fought where he had a quarter of a century before made his first stumbling steps as a military leader, that Stalin now rose to almost titanic stature in the eyes of the world." *Isaac Deutscher*, Stalin.

Left The Battle of Stalingrad. This was the most critical battle of the Second World War for the Russians. The defence of the city was essential if Russia was to defeat the Germans.

But this style of leadership served to heighten his mystique and prestige among the people.

In December Hitler suspended all operations for the winter. His troops had twice attempted, and failed, to capture Moscow. A bitter, harsh winter would take its toll on the Nazi forces. Already, Stalin planned a counter-attack.

But the mutual distrust between Russia and the Western allies held up their conduct of the war. Stalin was afraid in case a separate peace might be concluded in the West. He wanted the Allies to invade Europe and begin a "second front" against the Nazis. There was a bitter meeting between Churchill and Stalin in Moscow in August 1942. Stalin was informed that the second front had been postponed and that North Africa was instead to be the scene of the Allied invasion.

From now on, Russia had to go it alone. For Stalin, the turning-point of the war was the battle of Stalingrad. Between August 1942 and February 1943, the fate of the city, and of the Russian war effort, hung in the balance. The heroic defence of the city allowed Stalin to build up his reserves and prepare for a counter-attack led by Marshal Zhukov. The Germans were gradually pushed back. The Russians surrounded half a million German troops, led by von Paulus, and forced them to surrender. A tremendous victory had been won.

The Germans were now in retreat. In the summer offensives of 1943, the Red Army recovered vast areas of territory in the Ukraine. Although it would take almost two years before the Nazi regime was finally destroyed, there now seemed little doubt about the final outcome of the war. For the beleaguered Russian people, the tide was turning at last.

The supreme crisis of the system had been overcome. The will and determination of its people, no less than its material resources, had revealed the strength of the society that had been built under Stalin's leadership.

Yet the ideals which inspired the Russian victory were not socialist, but nationalist. Stalin deliberately encouraged a revival of Russian traditional nationalism. The values of the "fatherland" reigned supreme. "Death to the German invaders" was the most common slogan. Stalin even disbanded the *Comintern*, the international communist alliance, in order to appease his allies in the West.

Stalin could afford to take such measures. His reputation, both within Russia and in the rest of the world, had never been higher. The end of what would be known in Russia as the "Great Patriotic War" was in sight.

Above A German tank left abandoned in the snow after Hitler's retreat from Russia.

"**What, then, can we finally say of Stalin as a war leader? After his initial loss of nerve, he did hold firmly the reins of military leadership. Despite some tragic blunders, his basic ideas were in the end vindicated.**" *Alec Nove*, Stalinism and After.

12. The Fate of Europe

As the German forces retreated in the face of the advancing Red Army, Stalin's confidence and ambition increased. The international status of Russia, and Stalin's bargaining power with the Allies, grew also. The military campaign of 1943 saw the Red Army recapture two-thirds of the Soviet territory that had been lost to the Nazis. "The Red Army," Stalin said, "has become the most powerful and steeled of modern armies."

Stalin now had little fear that the Allies would make a separate peace with Hitler. Now that the defeat of Germany was almost inevitable, Stalin's main concern was to secure as many territorial gains as possible out of the settlement of the war. This concern was also shared by the other war leaders, Churchill of Great Britain and Roosevelt of the USA. In November 1943 the "Big Three" met at a conference at Teheran.

Stalin pressed Churchill to begin the "second front" by invading France, in order to take the pressure off Russia. Churchill, however, tried to palm Stalin off with promises of an invasion of the Balkans. But Roosevelt supported Stalin. At the end of the conference, the decision was taken in favour of an Allied assault across the English Channel. The Allies agreed that this assault—"Operation Overlord"—would begin in May 1944.

The statement of the "Big Three" at the end of the conference read: "We came here with hope and determination. We leave here friends in fact, in spirit, and in purpose." Yet despite this appearance of unity it was

> **"The results and consequences of the Red Army's victories are felt far beyond the Soviet–German front. They have changed the whole course of the World War and have acquired great international importance."**
> *Stalin, November 1943.*

Opposite page Having beaten back the Germans, Stalin's forces advanced into Germany itself. Here Russian troops raise the victory banner over the German headquarters in Berlin.

not long before the deep divisions among the Allies concerning the shape of post-war Europe became apparent.

After the Teheran conference, the stage was set for the political division of post-war Europe. The "Big Three" began to outline the spheres of influence of each country. Churchill agreed to the division of Poland that had taken place in 1940, in Russia's favour. It was provisionally decided that Greece should come within Britain's zone of control, and that Bulgaria and Rumania should be within Russia's.

The advance of Stalin's forces throughout 1944 made sure that the gains he stood to make out of this agreement were completely secured. The war front between Russia and Germany irresistibly shifted westwards. Poland, Rumania, Bulgaria and Hungary gradually came under the control of the Red Army. As long as the Nazis were the common enemy of all the Allies, Britain and the USA were powerless to prevent this extension of Stalin's domination of Eastern Europe.

Stalin, Roosevelt and Churchill met again, at Yalta, in February 1945. By this time, victory over Nazi Germany was within their grasp. The "Big Three" discussed the establishment of a United Nations Organization in place of the defunct League of Nations. The division of defeated Germany into various sectors was arranged. Stalin promised to join the war against Japan as soon as the war against Germany had been won.

By the last months of the war, it became clear to all that Russia was going to emerge from the war in a very strong position compared to the other combatants. Stalin set up "puppet" governments (controlled by Russia) in his various new satellite states—Rumania, Hungary, Poland and Bulgaria. In these countries the Communists used their control over the state machine to oust the old ruling classes and establish themselves in power.

At Potsdam, where the final conference of the victorious Allies took place, the suspicions of Britain and

the USA about Stalin's policies in Eastern Europe came into the open. The political division of Europe was now inevitable. The Western Allies were powerless to prevent it.

The victorious powers disagreed over their proposed treatment of Germany. At first they were pledged to maintain Germany as a unified country. But the Red Army's control of the eastern portion of the country led to its division into east and west regions.

This division reflected that of Europe as a whole. The creation of the "iron curtain" separating east from west would in later years be the main source of conflict between the major world powers. The war against Hitler had been won; but the Grand Alliance had already begun to fall apart.

Above Winston Churchill, Franklin D. Roosevelt and Stalin at the Yalta conference, 4th–11th February, 1945.

> "In an alliance the allies should not deceive each other. ... I as a naïve man think it best not to deceive my ally even if he is a fool."
> *Stalin, at the Yalta Conference.*

13. The Aftermath

Just over four years after the German attack on Russia, on 24th June, 1945, a victory parade held in Red Square celebrated the end of the Great Patriotic War. Stalin was acclaimed as the "Hero of the Soviet Union" and as the man who, almost single-handed, had won the war for his country.

It was widely recognized that the victory over Hitler had been made possible only by the intense efforts to industrialize the country in the previous decade. Stalin's policies seemed to have found their justification in the light of the great military successes of the Red Army.

Yet the cost of this victory was enormous. According

> **"Our victory means above all that our *social* system has won ... our *political* system has won."** *Stalin, 9th February, 1946.*

Opposite page A portrait of Stalin as Marshal of the Soviet Union.

Below The Victory Parade in Red Square, Moscow, 24th June, 1945.

to official sources, seven million people had died in the war, although the real losses were probably three times as many. Many towns and cities had been devastated by the conflict. Much of the countryside was ravaged by the rigours of war. Industrial plant had been destroyed. Millions of people were homeless, crippled and hungry.

A vast rebuilding programme was clearly essential. The war-weary Russian nation was faced with a task of a similar size to the one it had undertaken in 1929. But there was an important difference. From 1929 onwards, Russia was forced to industrialize without outside help. The country had only its own resources to rely on. But by 1945 Russia's domination extended over half of Europe. Stalin was able to use this domination to his advantage. Raw materials and industrial equipment were forcibly transferred from Russia's satellite states to help her industry to rebuild. Stalin was now in command not just of a single country, but of a whole empire.

The "iron curtain" which Stalin created was used to defend this empire from the influence of the West. The separation of east and west ensured that the millions of people under Stalin's authority would be isolated from "dangerous" Western ideas and culture.

The danger for Stalin was that the example of the higher living standards and political freedoms of the West could create discontent among his own people. In order to forestall such a possibility, the countries of Eastern Europe were rigidly controlled so that no information or publicity favourable to the West could seep through the "iron curtain". In addition, Stalin sponsored attempts to revive the traditional ideas of Bolshevism in order to cancel the "corrupting" influences of the capitalist West. By such moves, Stalin was able to ensure that the aftermath of war in his empire would pass without any serious challenge to his authority.

Opposite page The Dnieproges dam under construction.

14. The Last Years of Stalinism

In February 1946 Stalin announced the start of the first post-war "five-year plan". At the same time, he warned the country that three or more such plans would be needed before the peoples of the Soviet Union could achieve real security and comfort.

The Soviet Union had emerged from the war as the second most powerful nation in the world. Yet in wealth, industrial development and living standards, the country was still a long way behind the USA. In the last years of Stalin's rule, however, Russia was to make great advances in closing the gap between the two super-powers.

Despite the poor condition of much of the country's industry, and the weariness of its people, most of the targets of the five-year plan begun in 1946 were met. In the absence of the generation of young men who had died in the war, much of the heavy work involved was done by older men, women and even children.

The main reason for Stalin's intense efforts to expand the country's industry to ever greater heights was his fear of a future military conflict with the West. What became known as the "Cold War" had begun almost as soon as the Second World War had ended. America's possession of the atomic bomb—already used twice against the Japanese—made Stalin even more wary about the threat of a new conflict.

The Cold War began in earnest on 12th March, 1947, when President Truman of the USA announced that his government would intervene in any country threa-

> **"Stalin is the leader of world revolution. ... It is a great event that mankind is blessed with Stalin. ... Marx is dead and so are Engels and Lenin. Had there been no Stalin who would be there to give directions?"** *Mao Tse-tung, on Stalin's 60th birthday (1939).*

Opposite page President Truman of the USA. His attitude to Stalin's Russia in 1947 led to the start of the Cold War.

tened by communism. This so-called "Truman doctrine" was followed by the "Marshall Plan"—named after the American Foreign Secretary—by which the US offered economic assistance to those countries which were trying to rebuild after the war.

Stalin was suspicious about such policies, because he realized that they might appeal to elements in Eastern Europe who were unhappy with the new regimes. He resolved to reject the American policy and to clamp down even more tightly on the political life of the countries under his control. In this way he averted any threat of revolution in the east against the new Communist rulers. Opposition political parties in Poland, East Germany, Hungary, Czechoslovakia, Rumania and Bulgaria were suppressed, and the economies of these countries were brought under strict Russian control.

The Cold War was intensified by the dramatic events of 1948 in Berlin. Although the surrounding areas of the city were in Russian hands, the city itself was divided into zones controlled by the various Allied powers. In the spring of 1948, Stalin ordered a blockade of the sectors of Berlin controlled by Britain, France and America. But the Allies organized an air-lift by which food supplies, raw materials and fuel could reach the inhabitants of these zones. In the end, the blockade was unsuccessful, and the Allies retained their control of West Berlin. But the conflict between East and West had been brought to the boil.

The victory of Mao Tse-tung's revolution in China in January 1949 strengthened Stalin's position against the Western Allies. The following year the two leaders formed an alliance in which Russia undertook to assist in China's economic development. A few months later, the Korean War broke out. This ranged the main foes of the Cold War against one another in virtually open combat.

Yet in this conflict, as in others, Stalin was careful not to give the West any pretext for beginning a full-scale war on Russia. Peaceful co-existence was necessary as long as the economy was too weak to finance another long war.

But behind the "iron curtain", the process of modernization was speeding up. In the early 1950s the population of the towns in the Soviet Union grew by about 25 millions. Industrial output increased by 50% in the last four years of Stalin's rule. Alongside this industrial expansion, a new collectivization campaign was begun in rural Russia. In 1950, 240,000 collective farms were merged into 93,000 larger units. By this means Stalin hoped to counteract the chronic inefficiency of Soviet agriculture.

At the same time, by continuing his policies of political repression, Stalin made sure that the external threat represented by the Cold War was not accompanied by any attempted subversion within the citadels of communism. The defection of Tito's Yugoslavia from Stalinist control in 1948 was followed by the trial and execution of suspected "Tito-ites" throughout Eastern Europe, which recalled the mass purges of the 1930s.

Within Russia itself, censorship and propaganda were used to keep the people in line. Despite the difficult international situation, therefore, Stalin's dictatorship at home was as secure as ever.

In the early 1950s Stalin's health gradually began to deteriorate. Although before his death he never abandoned his control over the country's affairs, his potential successors began already to prepare their claims to power. Finally, on the night of 4th March, 1953, Stalin suffered his second stroke within a few days. At 9.30 p.m. on the following day he died at the age of 73.

> "Stalin spoke up about the atom bomb: 'That is a powerful thing, pow-er-ful!' His expression was full of admiration, so that one was given to understand that he would not rest until he too had the 'powerful thing'. But he did not mention that he had it already or that the USSR was working on it." *Milovan Djilas*, Conversations with Stalin.

> "Stalin died, and even his death compounded the atmosphere of mystery and terror. His successors feared universal panic, perhaps rebellion. The official communiqué lied about the place where Stalin had suffered the fatal stroke and died. The people were divided in their feelings between relief and fear of the unknown." *Adam B. Ulam*, Stalin—The Man and his Era.

85

Epilogue

To many people, the Soviet Union without the figure of Joseph Stalin seemed unthinkable. The writer Ehrenberg voiced the mood of these years: "We had long forgotten that Stalin was a mortal. He had changed into an omnipotent and mysterious deity."

Stalin's death was both the end and the beginning of an era for the Soviet Union. The loss of the leader who had ruled the country for such a long time was necessarily followed by a period of re-adjustment. Yet for many years after his death, Stalin's influence on the course of Russian history was immense. In Hingley's words: "During the two decades following the leader's death the Soviet political scene has been overshadowed by traumatic memories of his rule and has continued to be haunted by his ever-present ghost."

Stalin's impact on world affairs in the twentieth century has been second to none. In many ways, however, it is odd that Stalin should have had such an enormous influence. For it is widely accepted that his personal qualities were not those of a great leader. Stalin did possess shrewdness, cunning and a good tactical sense—and of course great ruthlessness. But as a thinker and writer he was unimaginative, as a speaker stolid and dull. Stalin totally lacked the spark of originality and the idealistic passion that appears to motivate the greatest of leaders.

It has been well said of Stalin that what was striking about him was that there was really nothing whatever striking about him. There would seem to be a glaring

> "Stalin's dark presence continues to hover over the Soviet Union and ... I fear that it will go on hovering for a long time. Despite the curses against his name, Stalin still lives in the social and spiritual foundations of Soviet society." *Milovan Djilas*, Conversations with Stalin.

Opposite page A *Punch* cartoon of 1956, showing Russians fleeing in terror as a statue of Stalin topples to the ground. The cartoon refers to the discrediting of Stalin by the Russians in 1956.

contrast between the unremarkable nature of the man and his remarkable achievements.

It could be said that Stalin's policies brought great benefits to the Soviet Union in terms of higher living standards, increased educational opportunities and so on. Yet these positive features of his rule cannot be separated from their gigantic cost in terms of human lives and suffering. It has been said that "Stalinism is one way of attaining industrialization, just as cannibalism is one way of attaining a high protein diet". Yet there have been some circumstances in which a resort to cannibalism is the only way for people in distress to remain alive. Whether Stalinism—with all its attendant horrors—was in some way inevitable as the path to modernization in the Soviet Union, or whether there was some other, more humane and democratic way, is an open question.

The life and work of Stalin is still a live issue today, many years after his death. His name continues to produce heated argument. This, as much as anything, testifies to the overwhelming importance of Joseph Stalin in the history of the twentieth century.

Opposite page A late portrait of Stalin

Morris J. Kallem
'43

Principal Characters

Berya, Lev (1899–1953). Head of the Soviet secret police (NKVD). Tried and executed at Stalin's orders.

Bukharin, Nikolai (1888–1938). Leading Bolshevik theorist and member of the *Politbureau* from 1918–29. Victim of a show trial and execution.

Kamenev, Lev Borisovich (1883–1936). Leading Bolshevik. Tried and shot in 1936 for conspiring against Stalin.

Khrushchev, Nikita Sergeyevich (1894–1971). Stalin's successor as first secretary of the Russian All Union Party. Deposed in 1964.

Kirov, Sergei (1886–1934). Member of the *Politbureau* and leader of the Leningrad Communist Party. Assassinated in 1934.

Lenin, Vladimir Ilyich (1870–1924). Marxist and leader of the Bolsheviks until his death.

Martov, Julius (1873–1923). Founder of Menshevism and leader of the Menshevik faction of the Russian Social Democrats.

Molotov, Vyacheslav Mikhailovich (1890–   ). Leading Bolshevik and disciple of Stalin. Soviet Commissar for Foreign Affairs, 1939–49.

Rykov, Alexei (1881–1938). Premier of the Soviet Union from 1924–29. Tried and shot in Stalin's purges.

Tomsky, Mikhail (1880–1936 or 37). Bolshevik trade union leader. Disappeared in Stalin's purges.

Trotsky, Leon (real name Lev Davidovich Bronstein) (1879–1940). Leader of the Russian Red Army. An enemy of Stalin, he was deported from Russia in 1929. Murdered by a Stalinist agent in Mexico, 1940.

Voroshilov, Klimenti Efremovich (1881–1969). Leading Russian military commander. President of the Soviet Union from Stalin's death in 1953 to 1960.

Zinoviev, Grigori (1883–1936). Leading Bolshevik, member of the *Politbureau* until 1926. Tried and shot.

Below Joseph Stalin in 1930.

Table of Dates

1879 Joseph Vissarionovich Djugashvili, later known as Joseph Stalin, born 21st December

1894 Stalin enters Theological Seminary at Tiflis

1898 Joins revolutionary group *Messame Dassy* (The Third Group)

1903 Russian Social Democratic Party splits into Bolshevik and Menshevik factions

1905 First Russian Revolution

1914 Outbreak of First World War

1917 February: spontaneous revolution causes Czar Nicholas II to abdicate

March: Stalin arrives in Petrograd, becomes editor of *Pravda*

April: Lenin arrives in Petrograd from exile

October: Bolsheviks seize power

1918 February: Treaty of Brest-Litovsk ends war with Germany

March: Russian Civil War begins

1919 Defeat of White Army in Civil War

1922 Stalin becomes General Secretary of Central Committee of Communist Party

1924 Lenin dies: Stalin combines with Zinoviev and Kamenev to defeat Trotsky in battle for Party leadership

1925 Zinoviev and Kamenev join forces with Trotsky against Stalin

1929 February: Trotsky deported from Russia

November: Bukharin removed from *Politbureau*

1933 Hitler comes to power in Germany
1934 Assassination of Kirov begins Great Terror
1936 Zinoviev and Kamenev executed after show trial
1938 Bukharin and Rykov tried and shot
1939 August: Nazi–Soviet Pact
     September: Germany invades Poland; Second
     World War begins
     November: Russo-Finnish War begins
1940 March: End of war against Finland
     June: French defences against Nazis collapse
1941 June: German invasion of Russia
     October: State of siege in Moscow
     December: Moscow relieved
1943 Teheran Conference of Stalin, Churchill and
     Roosevelt
1944 June: Allies invade Normandy; Soviet troops
     gradually occupy most of Eastern Europe
1945 February: Allied Conference at Yalta
     May: End of German resistance to the Allies
1947 Cold War begins
1948 Berlin blockade
1949 Korean War begins
1950 Pact between Stalin and Mao Tse-tung's China
1953 Stalin dies, 5th March

Further Reading

Alliluyeva, Svetlana. *Twenty Letters to a Friend* (Penguin, 1968). A close-up of Stalin by his daughter. Suitable for 11–16-year-olds.

Conquest, Robert. *The Great Terror* (Penguin, 1973). A thorough account of the mass purges of the 1930s. Suitable for older children.

Deutscher, Isaac. *Stalin* (Penguin, 1972). A detailed biography of the man and his time. Suitable for older children.

Djilas, Milovan. *Conversations with Stalin* (Penguin, 1968). An interesting account of several meetings with Stalin by a former Communist. Suitable for 11–16-year-olds.

Fischer, Louis. *The Life and Death of Stalin* (Jonathan Cape, 1953). A biography containing many insights on Stalin the man. Suitable for 11–16-year-olds.

Kochan, Lionel. *The Russian Revolution* (Wayland, 1971). A good narrative account of the origins and course of the revolution. Suitable for 11–16-year-olds.

Nove, Alec. *Stalinism and After* (Allen and Unwin, 1975). An informative work on origins and development of the Stalinist system. Suitable for older children.

Reed, John. *Ten Days that Shook the World* (Penguin, 1972). A vivid eye-witness account of the Russian Revolution. Suitable for 11–16-year-olds.

Trotsky, Leon. *Stalin* (Panther, 1969). A fascinating biography of Stalin by his great adversary. Suitable for older children.

Index

The author and publisher wish to thank those who have given permission for copyright illustrations to be reproduced on the following pages: Novosti Press Agency, 7, 11, 12, 15, 17, 20, 25, 26, 28, 32, 44, 49, 50, 52, 53, 55, 62, 65, 67, 68, 70–71, 73, 74, 77, 79, 81, 91; Radio Times Hulton Picture Library, 8, 14, 18, 21, 22, 24, 31, 34, 47, 48, 58, 59, 60, 61, 64; The Mansell Collection, *frontispiece*, 29, 35, 36, 39, 40–41, 42, 56, 78, 86, 89; Wayland Picture Library, 82.